The Hundred Lives

The Hundred Lives

Russell Thornton

QUATTRO BOOKS

The publication of *The Hundred Lives* has been generously supported by the Canada Council for the Arts and the Ontario Arts Council.

 Canada Council Conseil des arts
for the Arts du Canada

 ONTARIO ARTS COUNCIL
CONSEIL DES ARTS DE L'ONTARIO
an Ontario government agency
un organisme du gouvernement de l'Ontario

Author's photograph: Svetlana Ischenko
Cover painting: "Painting Number 200" by Wassily Kandinsky
Cover design: Sarah Beaudin
Typography: Diane Mascherin
Editor: Allan Briesmaster

Library and Archives Canada Cataloguing in Publication

Thornton, Russell, author
    The hundred lives / Russell Thornton.

Poems.
ISBN 978-1-927443-68-2 (pbk.)

    I. Title.

PS8589.H565H86 2014   C811'.54   C2014-904944-7

Published by Quattro Books Inc.
Toronto
info@quattrobooks.ca
www.quattrobooks.ca

Printed in Canada

And veering like a wind on the high seas,
the god approached as though she were already
dead, and instantly was there beside her,
far from her husband, to whom, with an abrupt
nod, he tossed the hundred lives of earth.

        — Rilke, "Alcestis"

Contents

With a Greek Pen

Night near Trikala   11
Oriste   12
Thessaloniki Train Station   13
A Woman and Child   15
Ouzo   16
The Shepherd and the Nymph   18
Larissa Gypsies   20
Flowers   22
Lemon Groves   23
Epidauros   24
The Cherry Laurel   25
The Monasteries of the Air   26
Larissa Baptism   28
Sappho's Moon   29
Hydra Great Friday   30
Turning the Lamb   32
Summer Snow   34
The Churches of Skopelos   36
The Seven Sisters   38
The Pathways Through the Apple   40
The Blood-Red Egg   42
Kefalonia   43
Larissa New Year's   44

Lazarus' Songs to Mary Magdalene

I   "I had left life behind, but even so…"   49
II   "When you knelt before him, and washed his feet…" 50
III "If you ask what it was like, I will tell you…"   51
IV   "When I took my first new, faltering steps…"   52
V   "It seems my body's wounds will never heal…"   53
VI   "Your tears, your vivid tears, fall like your hair.:." 54
VII "Because he had left everything but you…"   55
VIII "Because you love words, you made him summon…"   56
IX   "And when you finally lay with him nightly…"   57

from Book of the Dark Dove

Preface   61
"My brothers of the earth…"   62
"Where will I meet you…"   62
"Your eyes are doves…"   63
"He led me to a place…"   63
"As God could not fully…"   64
"She had drawn away…"   64
"She pours out…"   65
"I had abandoned myself…"   65
"O my love…"   66
"My beloved has entered…"   66
"She was swaying…"   67
"Her hair is black…"   67
"Here she sits…"   68
"Your name is the seal…"   68

Double-Flute

Pitcher   71
Letters   72
Canzoniere   73
Cells   74
Phone Number   76
Birds   77
Candy   78
Birthday   80
Anniversaries, End of August   81
A Stranger   82
The Smoke and the Fire   83
Cana   84
Absence   85
A List   86
Thirst   87
Double-Flute   88

Acknowledgements & Notes   90

With a Greek Pen

Night near Trikala

Back from an anonymous roadside village
where I sat outside beneath the brilliant skull of the moon
and ate plate after plate of food with friends
and talked and drank sharp Greek wine late into the night,
and wanted not to be alive at any time other than that night
and wanted not to be anywhere other than there,
where the conversation cornered me and invited me
to be exactly the person I was,
and to know a single unending instant of fine fury and delight
with logic and intuition flowing through me like wine,
I arrived at the small hotel where I rented a room
and found it locked for the night, and my door key lost,
and I slept on a bench in the central square
feeling as if I had drunk of the earth,
face to the voluptuous, cool, grape-dark sky
and the new stars with their millions-of-years-old light
that spread over me like glittering keys, like new senses,
and imagining I might never wake again,
or ever open the same eyes again, for they would go
making their own way in amongst people, in amongst gods.

Larissa

Oriste

In every market and shop and taverna
they are saying *Oriste! Oriste!*
meaning "May I help you?" or "At your service"
but not so nice or courteous-sounding —

literally, "I'm listening,"
and when translated into English
for the benefit of non-Greeks,
"What do you want?"

More assertion than question,
a word without wavering in it,
without pretence, without false graces,
like a perfect form,
like a marble column,
the sheer lines cutting the light.

Not a plea, not a prayer,
and still, a word like an act
of clear, hard love
for the God who is everywhere and does not exist,
who cannot be described or conceived of,
who is revealed in every stranger who walks in.
Oriste! What do you want? I'm listening.

Thessaloniki Train Station

We were on the train, waiting for it to depart,
and leaning out the window.
"Are you English!" he shouted at me. "I speak English!
"Thank you. It's a nice day!
Are you Yugoslav? I speak Serbo-Croatian!
Are you German? I speak German!"
And so it went, on and on. It seemed he knew
at least a few words of ten or twenty languages.
"Are you French? I speak French!
Are you Turkish? I speak Turkish!"
He was grinning, his face sweating and glistening,
standing as if at attention, talking non-stop to this audience,
surrounded by old suitcases, cardboard boxes, and paper bags
all spilling out the array of his belongings,
clothes, books, even small appliances,
and continually hitching up his woeful pants
that kept trying to fall down.

There were people from so many places on the train,
African students, Soviets of Greek descent
arriving in Greece for the first time, carrying caches
of hair combs to sell in the bazaars,
righteous young Brits and Americans with backpacks,
Dutch tourists, German tourists, Swedish tourists,
melancholy old Greek women, Greek families, Greek Gypsies,
and nervous, exhausted Albanians on the run –
and all had their ideas about who and what the man was.

Many claimed they had heard of him –
he had just gotten out of jail,
he had been a Greek government official and swindler,
he was a wealthy businessman on an alcoholic adventure,
he was a renowned gambler who had lost everything.
Everyone seemed to feel they knew him –
some even claimed he was a stand-up comic gone awry,
others recalled him as an ex-sitcom star.

"Are you Italian? I speak Italian!
Are you Danish? I speak Danish!"
He was harmless, it was just
that the different parts of whatever he called himself
were flying out in a hundred directions,
he was a wildly flashing switchboard,
he was the king bagman of the world,
living in train stations, on train platforms,
and sputtering out language after language,
he was the living ramshackle spirit of the tower of Babel
calling out to all the train passengers in the world
as to workers who could no longer understand one another
and were dispersing to come back and complete the labour
or the great tower would stay unfinished forever –
calling out because he saw how they were confused
and because in the same instant he knew
how they could feel certain of where they were going.

A Woman and Child

Sharp-eyed, in multi-coloured skirt
and high heels, with her free hand
she holds out roses and takes coins,
with the other, clutches and breast-feeds
her linen-swathed infant.

The instant collapses, and the clear
morning sunlight is a dream
of the foetus in the womb –
the watery mystery knitting
a lightning of flesh and bone –

now of the milk of eternity
suddenly flowing freely
over tables, into stalls, alcoves,
among clothing racks set up
along the aisles of the bazaar.

She draws her blouse, turns,
quick, musical speech on her lips,
and the world flashes, her earlobe's bangle.
Every word I have learned
goes after her, clinging to her neck.

Ouzo

You add water to a glass of ouzo
and a genie-less smoke rises in it asking, "What is it you wish?"
the ardent clear spirit distilled from the lees of wine
suddenly wreathed in opalescent fumes
and boiling away the sediment of your life and distilling the day
while you sit at a rough table in the mid-morning in front of the sea –
so you see there in the glass the vaporous myth of Plato's cave,
the man bound in chains, the theatre of shadows,
and beyond this, the sun's world-filling light.
And the day becomes simpler and simpler,
the day wakes you into light, you drink thick coffee,
walk and swim and sleep in the afternoon,
sit and wait for the blackness of the night to bloom,
the small brilliant white multitudinous flowers of the stars
to bloom from infinitely within the night's blooming.
And there is nothing here to wish for except what is –
nothing except the instant opening,
the sea clear as alcohol, the collapsed waves' foam bubbles
crackling along the sand like a delicate fire,
the distinct self-scoured sand grains, glasses of ouzo themselves,
and the nearby profusion of houses, all exquisite white words
strung around the hills, and the hills a smile of death.
And the old waiter who sets down the ouzo,
who makes his way without effort and with a strange beauty
around and around the perfectly arranged tables,
I see now he is the man who broke free of his chains
and walked out of the cave into the light of day.
It is as if he is the first person I have ever seen;
I do not know how it is that the wrinkles of his face
seem to multiply in the sun, nor how I now look at him through eyes
that are not mine, and he only smiles, for they are his eyes,
nor how it is that he is also young.
His eyes ask me what it is I wish, and he already knows
that it can be nothing except to wait for all blackness to deepen
and become one with all light, the hills here as they darken
and the sun's fire, come into clarity –

to wait for every question to return as an answer;
to wait to be placed in chains endless, transparent,
and travelling the absolute in flow.

The Shepherd and the Nymph
after seeing 'The Shepherd and the Nymph', a painting
by Themis Tsironis

With one outstretched hand balancing his staff,
and the other about to draw aside
the half of his coat still on his shoulder,
his shoes touching the silver-white water,
his eyes, large black drops, glowing, a half-smile
on his closed lips, the shepherd faces us
from across the stream.   A bird on a throne
of an odd-looking little mound of earth,
a bird in the upward fork of the limbs
of one of the environing thick-leaved
laurel trees, and a greyish hare, alert
to the ground nearby – look different ways,
and officiate.   Where the stream stretches
and runs up over and down a hillock,
she has stepped out to him, water splashing
and travelling brightly up her bare legs,
her transparent shift and never-combed hair
lifting out behind her – has leaned, and flung
her pale arms around him.   For the shepherd,
having in his solitude become pure
and inscrutable, an animal full
of God, and unaware of any day
other than the single day he lives in,
the one repeating round of dark and light,
she is what he knows most, is all he knows,
and yet visiting him for the first time –
the touch of the original desired
and desiring breath on him.

                    His eyes stare
past us and paint us as we did not know
we always were until now. The nymph's eyes,
though fixed on his profile, stare beyond him,
still of the stream that flows on past his shoes.
A fathomless love is there in those eyes –
though this is as if before time, before
anyone looked into another's eyes.

Larissa Gypsies

In the out-of-the-way taverna I come to every day,
a Gypsy family is eating an afternoon meal together,
the moustached father not looking up from his beans and bread,
the trio of shoeless children, all girls, preening themselves,
the young, worn mother looking away intently yet unfixedly.
Two passersby, other Gypsy women, stop,
turn their heads and launch an insult in across the handful of tables.
The young mother launches back an apparently inspired response
and instantly the exchange escalates into a full-blown verbal brawl.
The women outside begin shouting, spitting and making obscene
    gestures.
The woman inside begins shouting, spitting and making obscene
    gestures.
The taverna customers, the dozen or so of them, keep quiet,
until after some minutes a young man sniggers uneasily,
then another slips a glance at the taverna owner.
Suddenly, the taverna owner, fed up, marches up to the Gypsies'
    table
and orders, "Get out! Get out! Don't ever come back!"
The woman, however, is not paying him the least bit of attention.
Her husband, expressionless, is calmly eating,
her children are calmly putting the last of their food into their mouths.
Now the taverna owner, grabbing the woman, tries to remove her
    from her chair.
"All right, all right," she ends up relenting, "I'm going, I'm going,"
and finally stands up and walks out, husband and children in tow.
And now most of the taverna customers have stopped eating
and become an audience for the afternoon spectacle.
The taverna owner is out on the sidewalk shooing the Gypsies away,
while the three Gypsy women continue arguing, dancing around each
    other
and uttering forth a concoction of Greek, Turkish and Romany.
Even the Greeks, who have known Gypsy people all their lives, are
    awestruck.
These women, awkward and uncouth at the world's table –
they are the unbroken ones, never to be corralled,

fierce, free and playful out there in the air glistening as with their own
    gazes,
they are like winds from a wildly loved nowhere, laden with savage
    roses,
they are like living tarot scattered in the street.

Flowers
for Dora

No one could resist the charm in her bright black eyes.
The townspeople called her Little Maria.

You explained how her parents sent her out
to steal flowers she would then sell in the streets.

Now she was circling lightly through the bar
like an emissary, holding out a bouquet.

Had I drunk too much Greek wine, or had I seen
the same vivid Aegean-coloured flowers before –

left by the relatives who had come before us
to the graveside I visited with you that morning.

It was a year before, you had told me,
that you leaned over and closed your grandmother's blue eyes.

Lemon Groves

The horizon a burnt-out eye socket,
the sea a throng of mouths wounding themselves against sand –
the only shelter was inside the car,
so we drove down the peninsula just to drive,
until we came to a tract of green trees
running inland from the road and to the land's end.
We parked and went in amongst lemon groves,
vast, flowering lemon groves releasing fragrance for miles –
where we walked as if under the spell of the scent,
and where nothing could have been so apparent, so destined as this:
that within the scent-abounding white flowers
and the shade-giving leaves, lay the ripe lemons, the pert yellow
      spheres;
that within the fruit, within the sudden dream
arriving at the end of the way through the bewildering black
glare of the sun, shone the light of the lemon,
and we would stand finally in the bliss-shedding ray.
There, clasped beyond burning sight, we could dwell
in each other as in a single cool sanctuary
where whatever we knew of bitterness and hurt
could become the pure decision in us, nourishing and healing,
the secret, in the midst of burning change,
which would make us clear, clean-edged, purged of doubt.

Nafplion

Epidauros

The largest intact ancient theatre in Greece –
here I heard Cavafy's *Ithaca* recited
with the sun going down in the olive, orange, and lemon groves
that cover all the hills of the undulating horizon,
the sky filled with orange and yellow hues,
insubstantial chasms in the air of burning grief and rapture,
the sounds of the Greek words arranging themselves in the air:
Ithaca gave you the marvellous journey.
Without her you wouldn't have set out.
She has nothing left to give you now.
And if you find her poor, Ithaca won't have fooled you.
Wise as you will have become, so full of experience,
You'll have understood by then
What these Ithacas mean.
And then silence, pure crystal silence,
and stillness, sudden healing stillness,
by which the body may be made one with the spirit,
the sound unheard, the soul of all sound,
an Ithaca of silence, silence made manifest
through the sacred geometry of the theatre stone,
a Lady of Silence, of the secret of secrets,
energy unbound, which has brought forth every poem,
and every grief and union,
and which contains every as yet unwritten poem,
bodiless and radiant, as she is,
and waiting to enter into the circle of recited sound
and contain in itself stillness and silence.

The Cherry Laurel

The women who would gather in the vale
chewed cherry laurel leaves. When the poison
took hold and ushered them into frenzy,
they would see the vale was a hovering
of matter, a glittering haze. The earth
their bare feet danced on, and that had brought forth
everything around them, would, if they
threw off the names they had used for themselves,
begin to reveal to them what there was
of eternity in the world.
                    The vale
could open into a being, human,
yet other, whose name was a limitless,
pure embrace in an instant with no end;
then could close again and be a chaos
of innumerable identities
interspersed with abyss upon abyss.
It could pour blind currents of life, of death,
through the women's living skulls, and plunge them
into metamorphoses – so they might
suddenly know more than any mortal,
having become the vale itself, knowing.
Some would never return from such knowing,
and collapse and die. But others would now
be called Daphne, the name for the laurel,
and be priestesses.
                The light of the vale
is in love with those frenzied ones – the rays
sent as from Apollo still following
the woman who ran from him and escaped
when she was changed into a tree. The fate
of even Apollo's love is held here
in the laurel branches. Here, your own fate,
though you do not know that fate, now fills you,
while the light, the vegetation, and rock,
so bright, so mysteriously exact,
are a moving stillness about to speak.

Vale of Tempe / Larissa

The Monasteries of the Air

At the summits of isolated craggy pillars –,
the remains of eroded mountains
that stood at the edge of the Greek plain –
sit hundreds-of-years-old stone structures
like an uncanny unmoving gathering.
                                    We walk up
almost vertical interminable stairs
to the principal, still lived-in monastery, once
accessible only by rope and net.
                                    Here, a thousand feet
above tilled ground, the sun lets light
fall with great purity into scrupulous gardens,
doorways, clean stone paths.
                                    I follow others
into a museum displaying monks' icon work,
the code faces of saints and virgin and child,
and different medieval tools, and all the apparatuses
for hauling things up from below. The entire area,
we are told, was devastated during the last war,
but the monastery could not be touched,
and every monk took part in the resistance,
feeding people, hiding people.
                                    I enter a monk's cell,
a small cave, a stone nest for a man.
There is a cistern. There is a rough shelf in the rock.
How many fasted and prayed here, I wonder.
How many, in peacetime and in wartime,
fought to die before they died?
                                    There is a window
in the rock, and I lean my head out, look down,
and see the Thessalian villages sparkling,
and the fields of fruit and vegetables and cotton,
all seemingly spinning slowly. It is when
I turn, and face the cell interior again,
that I hear what I heard within the quiet
the first moment I stood here

without telling myself I heard it.
                                   What was it
that long sustained the solitary aspirant
if not this air, this ceaseless, breathy, hypnotic flow –
the cell is perched in it and contains it.
What was it that the aspirant learned
if not that he had to become a worshipper
of the measureless current, and pray to the praying air.
What was it the texts had tried to teach him
if not the unteachable secret in this air.
Here in his high poor cell, encased by rock,
encased by his body, with this air inside,
while the window blazed light, blazed darkness,
and blazed light again, hearing the air, he had
his more-than-definition of God, and his more-than-proof.

Meteora

Larissa Baptism

The child being baptized, not an infant but aged eight or ten,
had been born to a Greek father and a mother from a faraway
    country,
and because the father's family was well known in the town
the child was surrounded by a large crowd of people
that pressed close, curious to see the naked, shivering, shrieking,
half-foreign girl put into a metal tub full of water.
The priest, his tone unvarying, was reciting the ministrant words,
all the time swinging an incense-container back and forth on its
    chain,
sending out disappearing streams of scented smoke-mist.

The moist fumes and the echoey, huge-domed church air
suddenly turned cold, the cold of the air after a winter rain.
And it seemed to me I stood at a cold, thick-rushing creek
in a half-hidden ravine half a world distant from this place –
the grid of the suburban streets had been vanquished by fog,
and beside me, the fog travelling down through the ravine
had wound together all the trunks of the creekside trees.
And swirling and rippling around the random creek-bed rock, the
    creek water
was a white lustrous ore melting and running toward me.

The people, chattering, and coiffed and arrayed as for a TV camera,
and the bored-looking priest, were moving their mouths but were
    silent.
The child's crying was a wire of sound beyond hearing
that ran up the base of my brain, taut with strange terror.
Now the child would be received into the congregation –
I knew I would find, and not find, another, elsewhere.
I heard myself ask myself in my heart: Am I a child
or an old man? What am I that all I want to do is pray ceaselessly
to what I cannot know, to what may or may not know me?

Sappho's Moon

Eros, weaver of tales

— Sappho

A woman who is you and not you
is standing naked by the window,
the burden of her desire on her,
and the anonymous touch
of the moon, its soft dazzle
that is the story of light.
And she is asking that her desire
be woven into the story,
that she be released from her body
through her body and the moon's touch.
It is a night she knows she must wait
as if she has always waited
in front of a moon of waiting,
and the light made of distance
that brings the world to the world,
and the light made of her asking
to live in her life, that remains
as her desire grows outward
and twines with sorrow, and remains.
It is the light Sappho saw
and felt journeying through her,
shining now in the flesh of one
who is standing by a window,
and whose name I will not know
when I awake again beside her.
It is the story hidden in the flesh
that will tell us of the light
that shines from every form
in its elsewhere beyond desire,
but here must be woven together,
and her desire weave her a garment
of a subtle, endless cloth
that will wrap itself around her
and become her nakedness,
weaving a garment for the moon.

Hydra Great Friday

We are out walking, and go into a church
and take candles in our hands and light them
and go back out and join the procession,
the hundreds of others with lit candles
winding slowly through the hushed labyrinth
of narrow stone streets, the waiting blackness
opening around each arriving flame
and each held-out hand, each candle of bone
carried in its own dark within the dark.
The holy bier, the gold-embroidered pall
covered with all the flowers of the spring
bunched or woven into wreaths, and sprinkled
with lemon leaves and rose petals, passed this way.
The women are still here who threw incense
on vessels of embers and made the air
smell sweet as the bier passed before their homes,
icons of Christ crucified and white plates
of green barley outside their open doors.
We are silent, and I simply follow
and lead in half-ignorant reverence
through dark like layers of thick-falling soot
until we come to the sand of a small bay,
the procession now a large crowd gathered
where priests stand together in the water,
one swinging a censer on a long chain,
another reciting from a prayer book
a passage about repentance and death,
the words floating heavily back and forth,
back and forth across the air on the sea.
One steadies an effigy of Judas
on a pole, and when he lights it on fire,
its reflection loosens bright on the waves,
runs and touches at a shore of faces.
I stand at the back of the crowd and think
of no betrayer or man nailed to a cross,
but of how the beloved when they are gone

become the exact limits of those alive,
and edge the living loneliness, of how
the dead have died to send the sorrowing
out to their lives as to a procession
which will take them with others through a dark
as wide as the night and yet a prayer-niche
for any candle, for the eyes of any
making their way in a lit frame of bones
with all the holy dead to the first birth.

Turning the Lamb

It was my turn to sit and rotate the handle of the spit.
The whole lamb had been roasting since morning,
now it was glistening, juices trickling steadily out of it.
The lamb fumes thickened. I sat inches away
from the bed of coals, the heat in my face,
the brilliant white light of the Greek spring in my eyes,
looking out at you, your mother, your aunts, uncles, cousins.
Music had been put on, and was pulsing and blaring
into the walled space out back of your apartment,
and you and the other young women among your relatives
all took hands and began doing traditional dances.
As you went around and around, and back and forth,
you smiled and never let your eyes leave mine.
That was when your mother saw we were together
and called you a whore out of her eyes. And I thought
of her father the surgeon and Greek resistance fighter
starved to death in a blocked cave, of her husband
returning to his girlfriend a few weeks after her wedding,
and of the photo in her bedroom of you in her arms
when you were a baby. She would now do everything
she could to make me stay here, or to keep us a secret
while working at forcing me to leave. The day
continued, the lamb crackling, the music blaring,
moments reaching pitches of wild, uncanny joy
and boundlessness, moments immediately circumscribed,
quieted within the charged yet calm flow
in the circle of clasped hands. I took my turn
again, again. Everyone was drunk on Amstel beer
or village wine and half full on platters of french fries.
Finally it was time to gorge on the Easter Day meal.
One of the cousins sliced and piled on platters
unimaginably succulent pieces of the young lamb
to be circulated, and I sat and did not refuse to eat and eat.
Slowly the older ones headed into the apartment.
The younger ones, dazed and sleepy, followed.
All lay down in beds and on couches. I lay down in turn,

as I had sat to attend to the lamb. After a few hours
it was evening, and people rose and ate and drank again.
The music sounded different now, and I could understand
the Greek words and how the singer was drowning
and wanted to be thrown farther out to sea, was burning
and wanted more oil to be poured onto the fire.
The dancing resumed, the music grew loud and swerved
as the singer became more and more ecstatic, and I saw myself
still sitting near the lamb on its spit, as at a strict interface,
and shouted and pleaded within, slaughterer and slaughtered.

Summer Snow

I sensed presences, looked out the kitchen window,
and saw dozens of Gypsies in the backyard
sitting on blankets spread out on the grass –
all eating, talking, and looking in at me.
I went out on the verandah. Someone else
was there, a bearded man with an accent.
"Are they Gypsies?" he asked me. "Yes," I told him, "Roma.
    Gypsies."
"But many are White," he said. "Some have blue eyes."
"They're Gypsies," I said. "Believe me. I know."

The dream lit in itself a memory –
and I was out on a pier with a woman I loved.
I felt I had never been anywhere other than there.
"We're being watched," she said. "It might be best to leave."
I looked, and saw out on the nearby twin pier
a woman standing alone, straight-backed, radiant.

On the return ride along that shore,
with the air arriving heat-laden from the Sahara
blowing through the rolled-down car windows,
we had turned to stare at an enormous
fiery orange sun sitting in the sea, half-filling the blackening sky.
It flared and glittered in the circular hollow
sweeping through the froth the waves lifted and spun to the sand.
We saw, suddenly, a large party of Gypsies
camped on the beach, sitting outside trailers,
gathered together in front of a TV set.

Then the dream relinquished the memory,
and I was again at the kitchen window –
where I now saw no people but new snow lying in the backyard,
though it was the middle of summer.
I looked up and saw no cold white flakes floating down
but transparent glass circlets falling, displaying
unfathomable radial intricacies, ever-opening centres,

and falling as if not from clouds but a sun.
Then the falling flakes that were not flakes,
and the snow that lay on the ground, had disappeared –
or had become invisible, what I sensed in front of me unseen.
I woke seeing myself waiting at a window,
knowing I had waited here before and would again,
and knowing it to be a halting-place, yet a place
where every instant I was being informed
to gather up what I carried and depart.

The Churches of Skopelos

Waking suddenly in the island room,
the balcony curtain blowing aside
and flaring as if ablaze in the sun,
I heard a woman singing unaccompanied,
her voice so clear, the melody so strange,
so familiar, it was painful to me;
in her voice notes of sorrow, notes of joy,
were being gathered up in flowing flame,
and I concluded it must be a dream,
as I felt the singing in my body,
each part singing to every other part –
yet here I was wide awake. And I knew
what I was hearing was emanating
from some not far off church. And so I woke
the woman who lay asleep beside me,
and we dressed and went outside, where I heard
other church singing, and rhythmic praying,
all crisscrossing in the crystalline air –
but it was not what had awakened me.

We were at the base of a small steep hill,
the church nearest us was at the hill's crest,
we walked to it and listened at its door –
but here I could detect no sound at all,
so now we began following a path
of our own making from church to filled church
in slow, wandering search of her. We spent
the day in the lit hillside labyrinth
of winding streets, trying to find as many
of the two hundred churches in the town
of Skopelos as we could, some of them
in side streets like crannies, places only
the island's cats visited, some of them
anonymous in the hushed midst

of the blue and red house doors in cul-de-sacs,
some of them, cliff outcrops, radiant white
in the sun, like calm white birds in their nests.

At the last church we would come to, dozens
of people crowded around the entrance,
and they were all smiling softly; it was
as if we had found a celebration.
It was afternoon now, the sun pouring
down marble light, the shadows on the ground
black as black construction paper. We went
in where it was cool and evening-dark,
lit only by long thin hand-held candles,
and stood there in the small rough-hewn stone church
among those praying for the soul of a man
who had died a year earlier. The priest
was intoning from an aged large prayer book
open before him on its dark oak stand,
framed icons coated with gold, depictions
carved subtly in wood, and fathomless saints'
presences painted in primary colours
looked out at us from the whitewashed walls –
and no one sang here. Even so, I thought,
she must have sung her mysterious song
in the morning in a church like this one.

At the bright entrance they were handing out
pieces of honey cake, and they gave some
to the woman who had brought me to this place;
she touched my arm, gave me the cake in turn,
and I tasted its sweetness, happy, at home
in the gathering, among the mourners.

The Seven Sisters

You are beautiful, my love;
you are beautiful; your eyes are doves.
— Song of Songs 1:15

Telling worshippers and inquirers
the different messages that manifested
with the rustling of a massive oak tree,
with the clanging of tree-hung brass pots,
with the notes of a resounding bronze gong
set vibrating when a visiting breeze
touched a scourge one of you held in her hand;
interpreting the tinkling of cauldrons
hit by chains impelled by a wind; saying
in words what you could hear water saying
in the murmurs of a fountain; phrasing
the quick white-wingbeat-blurred movements of doves
in the oak branches —
                   you were the givers
of oracles, the sisters who founded
this sanctuary shrine, the ones called 'doves',
born from Pleione, who was Aphrodite
as Queen of the Sea, each an *ionah*,
name that had come from *yoni*, the Sanskrit
for the female genitalia.
                   Before
the dove of the masculinized Holy Ghost,
before the ethereal doves of saints,
there was the dove of the alluring one —
and there were you, the seven in the flock,
wild communicants of the world's structure,
of fullness of desire, whose utterance
loosed the insistent, always close unknown,
letting every asker's question widen
as that question's answer enfolded it

in incalculable vitality,
in pure question.
                      You were the seeresses
of the body, whisperers and chanters
in continual contact with the earth,
the dove-priestesses of an inner eye,
eye between the feathery labiae,
or eye, omphalos and eye, flanked by doves,
sign of the world's centre – prophetesses
of an inner touch in search of the touch
of the greater body and its desire
within which human desire was answered
as if from beyond death, from a cluster
of hundreds of brilliant stars surrounded
by a nebula, and named after you,
the Pleiades, the 'flock of doves'.
                           Bright, dark dove,
eye of desire, oracle of the light
of lights that is dark, oracle and eye
of vision beyond sight, emblem of touch,
and of all things calling out to all things,
yoni and luminous-hazed star cluster,
you are beautiful, you are beautiful.

Dodoni

The Pathways Through the Apple

So when the woman saw that the tree was good for food,
and that it was a delight to the eyes, and that the tree
was to be desired to make one wise, she took of its fruit and ate;
and she gave some to her husband, and he ate.
— Genesis 3:6

after looking at a book of religious art

The depictions in the paintings all tell
the accepted story: the temptation
and fall took place when the primordial
woman listened to the exhortations
of a serpent in a beautiful tree,
and ate of the apple, the forbidden
fruit of the tree, and offered it in turn
to her mate.
          But Gypsies say the apple
is holy – its holiness arises
from the sign at its core, the natural
pentacle, the secret five-pointed star.
They say the way to cut an apple
is transversely – so it reveals its secret –
especially when it is being shared
between lovers.
          That inner apple star,
that knowledge, if it is hidden and sacred,
it is hidden in the flesh of the apple
as the maiden is in the old mother,
as the virgin is in the holy whore,
as she who has never chosen a mate is
in the repeatedly wedded one –
as the bride is in the pictured woman
who offers her groom the holy apple,
his death within it, his transformation,
and return to paradise.

                    The pathways
through the apple will lead him – and the loved
and loving bride be both those pathways
and the garden the groom is going to,
and the two become one know the marvel
of the flesh that has come into existence
because of the spirit, and the marvel
of marvels of the unfathomable
spirit that has come into existence
because of the flesh.
                    That bright held-out fruit
the bride's simple signalling to the groom
of the mystery within the two of them
that will lead him along pathways – as along
the branches of the invisible tree
by which the world arrives at each instant –
and bring him to where a man and woman
are forever being re-created
between new meetings and new farewells,
unknown to one another and yet twins
in the midst of the presence in the field
of shining, eternally laden trees.

The Blood-Red Egg

When she saw and spoke to the risen Jesus, she hurried off
to tell the other disciples. On her way, she met Pontius Pilate
and told him the wondrous news. "Prove it," Pilate said.
At that moment a woman carrying a basket of eggs passed by
and Mary took one in her hand. As she held it before Pilate,
the egg turned brilliant red.
– from a traditional story about Mary Magdalene

after seeing 'Mary Magdalene', a painting by Themis Tsironis

The way the water changed into wine
so the wedding could continue, and widen,
the way the two loaves and five fishes
multiplied five-thousand-fold –
a woman holds out an egg before a judge,
and the egg turns brilliant red.
It is as if she has taken the place
of the performer of miracles,
the one she has given all her love to,
and she holds out and reveals
the woman's egg she has found
in the basket of her body,
the egg of his birth in the other world.

For her part she knows every man
asks that he be seen as he truly is,
though the instant he is seen
he is a miracle, an image risen
out of the seer and seen now one.
The two disappear as into a circle
they make moving round each other,
all proof moving round all proof,
as into an event that never ends,
where a man and woman become dust
and dust becomes a man and woman
in a field of vision they themselves are,
widening, narrowing, widening,
and lit with images, wondrous news.

Kefalonia

There, they tell how the origin of the island's name
is in the sound of the name and what it carries of the island's beauty.

There, you turned to the low bridge that stretched across the bay.
"Why not a road around?" you asked, mathematician, engineer,
    finder of solutions.

While we were out on a balcony, where you could be in the full sun,
I watched a man perform a balancing act up in the air –

in bright black walking shoes, dress shirt, dress pants,
he was working on a nearby roof, replacing ruined or missing tiles,

preparing a house for the wind and rain that would arrive in winter.
Then, out on the deck of the ferry on the way back to the mainland,

we stood at the stern alongside a man facing the island and waving.
"He's going far from Kefalonia," you said, staring through the wake.

"Send me your homemade bread!" the man shouted to shore.
The people seeing him off, unhearing, went on waving as before.

There, you had travelled far from your name, and the meaning of the
    name
held you no more than an opposite – you were 'God's gift', you were
    'one God was taking away'.

And you had travelled far as from a home to which you would never
    return,
and had come to a place where you had eaten the honey, the quince
    paste,

drunk the white wine, and walked the hills breathing the scent
of the cedar-like fir trees that grow nowhere else in the world,

and which you were now leaving. Now the name of that place
could have no meaning for me except in what it would carry

of the person you were – in what it would keep in its sound
of the beauty that knew itself as you. On that island, on Kefalonia.

Larissa New Year's

If you were lucky, you said, by the end of the night
we would have the money for a holiday
on Evia or Alonissos, on Thassos
or Halkidiki – or we could even go to Crete.
All New Year's Eve you beat men at cards –
one by one they exited the game.

I sat back at the bar and watched
and thought of the night we had met,
when you stated you foresaw deaths
then tried to forget – the neighbour, the relative,
the stray kitten you introduced to a mother
and her brood that hissed it away.

And you told me you were a thief. I admitted
I, too, had stolen things – for a time –
but now to find metaphors was to pocket
new money. I wanted to steal a thing
from its class and marry it to an alien other.
You nodded at that – all contradiction,

calculating, vicious in an instant,
yet frightened and soft-hearted
in a way you had to hide. People either died on you
or deserted you. But I had no choice –
I had to stay to see the constant startled look
in your green eyes, to see you perform

your ritual behind a half-closed kitchen door
with olive oil and floating flame
to keep away the evil eye, to see you dab
holy water on your throat in crazily driven taxis,
to see how you stood as at an interface
where gods and goddesses appeared.

Nicotine addict, gambler, who thieved
everywhere, who also gave without thinking,
you foresaw nothing of the thief
who came for you yourself. Or did you?
Every holiday you took, you might have half-meant
to lose him in a lit street. That startled look,

you sensing he had begun his work in you –
the way you somehow knew what cards
were in players' hands. What I knew was the cutting
of the New Year's Day cake going wrong,
the coin wrapped in waxed paper not to be had
by you or me that year – and then, not any year.

Lazarus' Songs to Mary Magdalene

I

When Jesus saw her weeping ... he groaned in the spirit,
and was troubled.
— *John 11:33*

I had left life behind, but even so,
when he called I could hear his hidden longing,
and I knew it was the fierce, clear brightness
of his longing I felt rise like dawn through my blood.

His voice hurt me, his calling me to come out,
to take breath again, commanded the same sickness
that had ruined me to fill me again,
and it was as if coming back was another death.

The common shroud I had been buried in
had come unwound, revealing my bandages,
which were filthy, and hung off me like rags.

I was covered in open wounds. These wounds
were now my eyes, and through them, light saw you,
arraying you in every story of love.

II

It was Mary which anointed the Lord with ointment ...
whose brother Lazarus was sick.
— John 11:2

When you knelt before him, and washed his feet
with your tears, and dried them with the hair of your head,
and anointed him with precious ointment,
that was when my own destiny began.

Your hands on him, and your worshipful lips
kissing his feet, were a slow and desperate
prayer of love beneath all silences.
I knew he would love you like no other.

When he said to his disciples to take
the stone away from the grave in which I had lain
dead and rotting for four days, he did so

because he could no longer withhold his love for you,
and because to him the world had become a door
which opened and let him seek the world and find himself.

III

Jesus saith unto her, Woman, why weepest thou?
Whom seekest thou?
— John 20:15

If you ask what it was like, I will tell you:
I knew I had no eyes with which to see,
no ears with which to hear, and knew nothing
else, not anything of whom I had been

in life, and not any feeling at all
until he called. It is only now, having come back,
that I have a vision of a man and woman –
they are embracing with infinite care,

and now they are shattering in each other's arms,
and the pieces of them are the fragments
of a shattering brilliant mirror.

Each piece seems to be crying out "I love you,"
but the man and woman have disappeared,
and the words are the dazzling, soundless light.

IV

And he that was dead came forth ... Jesus saith unto
them, Loose him, and let him go.
— John 11:44

When I took my first new, faltering steps
into the midday light, I stepped into his love.
I knew in the strangeness of my body
he had asked himself who it was he loved.

And I knew he had sent his love down into rock,
tracing all the agony of his love
back down to its root, back down to deep rock
where there were no names, no him and no you.

I knew he had asked himself how it was
that he had refused you. For his refusal
had been useless; the chains he felt imprisoned in,

and felt were somehow you, were his own flesh,
his own marrow. And if he let himself
become those chains, the chains would melt away.

V

And there was a certain beggar named Lazarus,
which was laid at his gate, full of sores.
– Luke 16:20

It seems my body's wounds will never heal,
for they close only to open and bleed again –
it is they that are immortal in me.
The pain, too, I know will live forever.

Often I dream that invisible birds
are perched in the recesses of my wounds –
they come and go as if I sent them out
like the raven and the dove. Is the soul an ark?

When his soul learned touch, discovering the missing
parts of itself in your body, it came ashore
in his body and touched his deepest dream.

You effaced him then in the syllables
of his never having seen anything but you,
and slowly you named him as you are named.

VI

... she hath washed my feet with tears, and wiped
them with the hairs of her head.
— Luke 7:44

Your tears, your vivid tears, fall like your hair,
the long and sweeping down tresses of your hair —
always you are trying to catch your tears
with your upturned and waiting, bewildering

fingertips, and somehow hold your tears close,
and take them to yourself, as if they were children,
as if they were orphans, and they themselves
were weeping to be chosen, to have a home.

Like your tears, travelling and lost in you,
like your tears, trying to return to you,
he, too, was trying to find you, and he

would pray to his hands to invent themselves
so he might at last find that the doves he knew
were crying beneath your skin and seeking his hands.

VII

And he turned to the woman ...
– Luke 7:44

Because he had left everything but you,
because he had shed everything he knew to shed
beside you, you showed him he had not yet begun.
He felt his blood, but it was not enough:

beyond his blood, beyond his hidden self,
he sang to you as a wave at its height,
the wild, locked-in, sourceless grief breaking free,
the bright foam erupting at the wave's tip –

a thousand saviours' cries of abandonment –
and this was the moment of both fury
and peace when he was one with you at last,

when the two of you were changed, were no longer
who you knew yourselves to be, having unclothed
yourselves of all beginnings, all endings.

VIII

Because you love words, you made him summon
what was wordless and suffering in you
into the nakedness of his own eyes.
All the words he said, gentle, powerful —

they did nothing if they did not call out
their claim on you, but could never claim you
any more than he could claim eyes, or claim the sight
that eyes find, when to see you was to know

it was you who looked out through his pupils' blackness.
For him you were the only one in whose
shining, searching eyes sorrow had concealed itself,

as if ashamed of its eternity,
so he might see your eyes as beautiful
if he prayed to words to let him see beyond them.

IX

And the twelve were with him ... and certain women ...
Mary Magdalene, out of whom went seven devils ...
– Luke 8:1-2

And when you finally lay with him nightly
and with your body burnished his body,
it was not unlike dying; and when you
made his body incandescent, and ignited it,

you who had brought your drunken heart to him,
you who had always been one who waited
as if water thirsted, as if new bread hungered,
you turned him into fire, and his soul rode the fire.

You extinguished him in the harmless flames
that weave the world's scattered parts together,
you let him burn within that composure

that is your unutterable beauty,
that is the colourless eye of the world,
you let him feed it like inexhaustible oil.

from Book of the Dark Dove

Preface

These pieces are excerpts from a longer work, *Book of the Dark Dove,* imagined as a Latin text dated the late 14th century, the work of an unknown author, and discovered in the mid 20th century in the basement of a church near Florence.

Most of the text consists of elaborations on lines of the *Song of Songs* in the voices of the speakers of those lines. There are two main speakers in the *Song,* the Bride (the Shulamite) and the Bridegroom. A number of the sections of the text are responses in one of the two main voices in the *Song* to lines spoken by the other. Some sections of the text amount to glosses on the *Song.* In other sections the text is a fiction in its own right, with lines of the *Song* serving as points of departure.

Bride: *My mother's sons were angry with me.*
They made me a guard of the vineyards;
my own vineyard I did not guard.

My brothers of the earth seized my vulva. They violated me. They broke me and divided me from my state of oneness with the king. My mirror was shattered and my light lost. Where my vineyard was a field bringing forth God, now it was a darkness obscuring God. They made me the accused one, the spurned adulteress, the profane harlot. They then made me a guardian of chastity. Night and day I guard the vineyards. God does not taste men, and men do not taste the wine of God. I guard the vulvas of the harem, when my own vineyard I can never guard, as it is open to all who utter praise: *I am the first and the last. I am the honoured one and the scorned one. I am the whore and the holy one. I am the wife and the virgin ... I am she whose wedding is great, and I have not yet taken a husband ... I am the utterance of my name.*

Bride: *Where do you pasture?*
Where do you let your sheep lie down at noon?
And why should I be as one veiled
among the flocks of your companions?

Where will I meet you? Where is the sacred sheep-stall where you will unite with me? Where will your lady of the flock find you? Where will they not see me wrapped in the harlot's garment? Tell me where I must take my vulva. O my beloved, I long to meet you. Follow me to the sacred stall. The he-goats will inspire you. Follow me into the stall of vision and love, into the secret darkness in the glare of the sun. Follow me into the invisible.

Bridegroom: *You are beautiful, my love,*
you are beautiful.
Your eyes are doves.

Your eyes are doves. They are dove-shaped. They are doves. Your eyes are dark. They contain the light of lights. Your eyes ask for love. They shine brightly with love. Your eyelashes, like canopies, lay shadows beneath the gentle clarity of your gaze. Your eyes are purity, sweetness. They are the eyes of desire. They are dove-shaped. They are doves. Your eyes are yoni-like. Your eyes are dark. They contain the light of lights. Your eyes ask for love. They shine brightly with love. They are doves. The yoni is a dove. The yoni is the inner eye. It is the eye of vision beyond sight. It is the eye of rebirth. Your eyes are doves. They are dove-shaped. They are doves.

Bride: *He brought me into the wine-house;*
his intent toward me was love.
Sustain me with raisin cakes,
refresh me with apples.
I am faint with love.

He led me to a place of love, of exultation and joy. His erection brushed against me. I bent over a large clay jar and sipped wine through a tube while he had me from behind. Let us eat sweet raisin cakes made in the shape of the goddess. The goddess will preside over us. Let us eat apples. Refresh me with apples, my love, the apples of union with the powers of life. Support me, restore me, so our love-making may be long and repeated.

Bridegroom: *O my love, in the crannies of the cliff,*
               in the covert steep,
               let me see your face, let me hear your voice.

As God could not fully reveal himself to Moses, and showed him instead the lit bush, so you cannot fully reveal yourself to me. As doves hide in the clefts of the mountain rock, so you hide from me. And then in the arms of sleep, I dream I am in a valley of doves. The valley ends as a wild pass closed in between two sheer rock walls. Suddenly a flock of thousands of doves appears with a rush and whir that is like a gust of wind.

Bride: *Catch us the little foxes,*
          the little foxes that ruin the vineyards –
          for our vineyard is in blossom.

She had drawn away from me, flirting with me. Catch us the little foxes, she whispered, flushed and sheened in sweat, a smile on her lips, challenging me, urging me. Ravage the vineyard, ravage it like the foxes with fire in their tails. Let its blossoms be torn, let it be ruined as by the foxes that Samson sent running through the vineyards, torches tied to their tails, setting the vineyards alight.

The vineyard burns up before him, and illuminates the hidden one, the honoured and scorned one, the drunken one, the daughter of the vine, the wine, and the full wine-glass at his lips, the light of lights which is dark, dark grape dark, which he, wild and boundless with boundless touch, tries to utter, and is now addressed by: Let us be drunk with its dark wine, let us know the smile of the wine.

Bride: *Upon my couch I sought him whom I love;*
          I sought him but did not find him.

               *   *   *

          When I found the one I love
          I held him and would not let him go
          until I brought him to the house of my mother,
          to the chamber of her who conceived me.

She pours out a lament, the queen of loss and death. And now she must search through the darkness to find her lover. "Do not disdain me," she pleads. "Do not cast me aside. I am with you in the depths of the darkness, and although my nature is hidden, if you hear me, if you reach out to me, I will be for you the morning star." Only when she finds him will he be able to redeem her, and her brilliance shine forth for him. Only when she finally clasps his hand, and leads him to the temple, will she be able to heal him of ravages. And only then will he know her love, and how she looks on death with smiling, immortal eyes.

Bridegroom: *You have ravished my heart, my sister, my bride,*
               you have ravished my heart
               with a single glance of your eye.

I had abandoned myself in order to see you. I had prepared myself to assume the condition of a slave. This was my labour. One encounter, one glance from you, and I was wounded, and knew my emptiness. At the same time I was emboldened. You made my heart rise. I had been seen by the other, the eye of the Beloved. When beauty looks forth, love appears beside it. When beauty shines, love lights its torch from the flame.

Bride: *The watchmen who patrol the city found me.*
           They struck me, they bruised me.
           The guards of the walls stripped me of my mantle.

O my love, I beheld you at the moment you beheld me. I, too, was wounded. I, too, was possessed by desire. But you are one of the watchmen, and one of those who tore away my garment of holiness, when out of love I had come to you. You impeded me in my search for you. You, along with the others, struck me.

Bride: *My beloved has gone down to his garden,*
           to the balsam beds,
           to feed in the garden, to gather lilies.

My beloved has entered the other world. He is in the embrace of the heavenly bride. He is in union with the goddess. My beloved has entered paradise. He is in the womb of vision. Through my vagina, my beloved has gone down to the beds of spices, to the realm of the soul.

Bridegroom: *Turn, turn, O Shulamite,*
                turn, turn, and let us gaze upon you.

She was swaying before the altar, chanting. As she moved, the veils concealing her lifted and revealed long tresses. Silver and turquoise bracelets adorned her arms and ankles. A highly crafted chain encircled her neck, and below it an ornament studded with lapis lazuli hung upon her breast. Around her waist was an embroidered girdle. She began to dance to the music of the flute, the tambourine, and the cymbals. As she danced the contours of her form were revealed under her almost transparent robe. With her every movement she radiated love. She did not look at me. She was alone. And yet she was making herself receptive, preparing to open to me. Her dance was a dance of two worlds. Her movements were a bridge across which I could walk as into a dream, and yet be more and more fully awake.

Bridegroom: *The locks of your head are like purple;*
                a king is held captive in the tresses.

Her hair is black, violet-black, rinsed in the dark wine colour of dye, the holy purple. Her hair imprisons me as in a maze. It casts me into frenzy. It burdens me with yearning and uncertainty. Love has branded my heart with the swirling letters of her curls. Each ringlet has within it fathomless charms. I am entangled in beauty and calamity. I am lost. I cannot find my way. Her hair is the beauty of the manifested world. It is the veiling of the divine essence. It is the multiplicity of the creation which hides the unity of all things, and it is the concealing of the non-existence of all things. Her hair is numberless worlds, and is abyss upon abyss. Curl within curl is an endless story, an endless explanation. Each curl is a twist of fate. Her tresses all in disarray fall upon me in myriads. I seize a single strand. It is a suspended chain. It is the chain of vicissitude, and it is my guide.

Bride: *I would give you spiced wine to drink,*
          the wine of my pomegranate.

Here she sits, offerings of little boats filled with vivid flowers laid at her feet. Enthroned with her holy child on one arm, she holds a pomegranate, a symbol of the fertile womb, with its dark red juice and numerous seeds. These are the seeds, it is said, eaten by virgin mothers who conceived saviours. This is a forbidden fruit, the apple of seeds, each with one seed from the garden of Eden. Our Lady with the pomegranate, when a man performed the role of your lord and bowed at your shrine, and drank of the wine made of the juice of the pomegranate, he let his familiar senses die. His inner senses were then reborn in you. He drank of what is within the seeds of metaphor, which marry life to death and death to life. These are the seeds of the continual conception through the bride of the child, who is the god of the poem, and the always unborn poem of poems.

Bride: *Let me be a seal upon your heart,*
          like a seal upon your arm;
          for love is as strong as death,
          passion as mighty as the netherworld;
          its flashes are flashes of fire,
          the blaze of God.

Your name is the seal upon my heart, and the writing on the seal. Your name is a shield against death, and the writing on the shield. Your name is as fierce as death, for it is the name of death as it is the name of life. Your name is the name of love. The desire you excite in me is as powerful as the pull of death, and beyond it, for its fire is of the fire of God. Within the fire of my love for you, and within the ashes of my body, is the hard gem of love. Within the fire is the diamond body, the jewel in the depth of my being. Within the fire is you, the one ornament of all being.

Double-Flute

Pitcher

Entering her parents' house in secret,
finding a pitcher of ancient design
sitting on a plain wooden shelf. Knowing
that moment in the dream that she has died
and time has passed. No one having told me.
Then going with the pitcher in my hands
out into the vague street. Great energy
beginning to flow through me. The smooth loop
of the small handle. The quick curve and gleam
to the base. The soft plummet at the mouth.
The dark space within will urge me on now
and I will see that it is desire vast
and wild as death, and it hid here before
it came to break me, and is filled with her.

Letters

I threw away your letters.
Years ago, just like that.
The tight black swirls,
circles and strokes
filling fine sheets –
I would not see them again.
The last items I had left.
The dates. The phrases.
The things you said. Forfeited.
Snowflake patterns.
Leaf diagrams.
Crushed. Melted. Dissolved.
The flooding runoff
at the backed-up
street corner drain
collects it all.
Only the opening
of a strong seal far below
could allow that pool
of darkening rainwater
to run and drop away
between the slats.
If I were to recover
the lost key of the cursive,
I would in one instant
want back again what I saw
in the images
the hand traced out for me.
And would be denied
even the little
the letters kept of you
and be released
into nothing but more time.

Canzoniere

Smoke from a Petrarch sestet
rises off the deep white page.
The fire still burning the dark,
inexhaustible fuel
flowing within the metre,
the consonants, the vowels.
The carbonaceous product
of the lines arrives nowhere
except at its end in air.
Martyrdom will not allow
the singer to heave to shore
before he is lost in fire,
before he is trackless smoke.

In the heart of the atom,
there too, the particles die,
are reborn a thousand times,
no longer exist, exist.
In the emptiness, other
fates beyond the name of fate,
other smoke and other fire.

Cells

I find webpages and see the faces
of two of your now forty-something siblings,
and imagine how you looked in middle age.
Study even the obituary notice picture
of your mother, seventy-eight, for clues.

But you are twenty-two. It is late summer,
you are wearing white pants, a simple blouse,
you stand at a distance and smile slightly,
and let me take a photograph of you.
You are there in sunlight, in my cells –
you are there, you are twenty-two.

Meals I did not sit and eat with you,
and my food and drink without you now,
all of it nourishment for the cells –
the cells vanished along with what they held
of what I was and what I knew of you
and since replaced with new cells,
and the cells still here, which will vanish.

I saw somewhere among a poet's lines,
What is not of flesh, we won't remember.
And I know that the cells of the body
both remember and disavow the body.
And the living flesh is its testimony
that it can only remember then forget.
And the sunlight falling all around you
is timeless, blameless, and continues falling.

And what is of the body, we will remember
because it is what we can possess, though it can't last.
And what is not of the body, if we imagine
it is another body that can only remember –

even then it can't save us. The body will forget us,
and if the spirit can tell us it knows us,
or which among the scattering and fading cells
comprised us, we won't be there to hear it.

Far inside the cells of my body now,
where I am only barely a body, in sunlight
you are twenty-two, and you remember and forget,
and you arrive neither to fulfill touch
nor invisibly hold sway, and you step toward me.

Phone Number

Your phone number reminded me of your hair.
I don't remember it. I remember the blackness
in the run of the numerals in print and in my ear.
I remember your hair. I was in a phone booth.
I was young, drunk. The numbers stayed slurred.
Your hair was the blackness outside the glass.
The strands of it wound black through the street.
The black stamp of your hair was all over me.

The electronic tones echo as I swipe a card
and try sequence after sequence of digits.
I ask for you among people I don't know.
In the hollow I hear my heart vibrate and pump,
pressing its own keys, all blank, again and again,
all correct for the connection to go dead.

Birds

Three decades gone, and I have paid nothing
against the arrears of my life but time.
The interest, the interest on the interest,
on a moment that lit a deep, soft dark
is taking me ever farther away
from what I feel are still flying to me,
the silent melting birds of your mouth.

Candy

I

When they put tablets on each other's tongues,
knowing it was time, and the young woman
gave a tablet to their child, saying to him
over and over, stroking his hair, sleep,
and they lay down, the small child between them,
they interlaced in quietness and stillness
that conquered all circumstance, they tasted
the worst anyone could taste and then even
when their eyelids lowered as if weighted
and the capability to speak left them
and they were being swept into nullity,
they continued to resist, they touched hands
across their dead child the moments before
the men with guns aimed at them forced the door.

II

They lay again where they lay together
the first time, sharing within kissing mouths
crimson glaze-coated confectionary,
laughing as the pieces melted through them,
they lay in the long viridescent grass
gazing into the deep blue forever
of the sky, the sky a door open wide,
a white cloud floating by, they lay again
where they turned together and were ushered
into the original flesh of pure faith,
and the day they lay there and their last day
were one and were what they knew now of days,
and this day alone lifted and carried them
beyond division of future and past.

III

Then when the two could no longer hold on
and their hands fell away from one another,
they were taken up in a wild waiting,
a desiring outside all categories
of thought and feeling that was also an act,
a withdrawing into itself, a filling
itself again in grass, sunlight and air,
as in a never ending birth, neither
bitter nor sweet, that they in human love,
the love the end that it begins, crystallized
in the flesh as what was sweet, cancelling
what was bitter, they were gone, they were the way
they had known the sweetness, they were the candy
and the way they had known the touch, the candy.

Birthday

You had lived less time then
when we knew one another
than I've spent recalling you.
I know almost nothing of your life
between the time we spent
together and when you died.

That day, your birthday, when
you sat with me, wearing a red
angora sweater, red lipstick,
your hair shining black, I said,
understanding only a little,
"You are an Etruscan young woman."

In catacombs I visited years later,
when I saw the smiling women
of the sculptures of couples sitting
on tombs, I saw them painted
with crimson clothing and lips,
and this gave the darkness its glow.

Anniversaries, End of August

Anniversaries circle round again. My grandparents
marrying in the sun. The guests in their best attire.
The filled vaulted room. Then the clinking glasses.
Then the private rites of those who waited long.
It is there in the light. Light that is a window.
And is a mirroring sea for my grandmother
out in the sailing ship of her wedding dress. Her ashes.

Someone I loved dying alone. The month the wide frame
of her final leaving. It was also her birth month. Light
opens its window, and is window upon window.
Her living hair darkens beyond its living black.
That black is another light, no visible sun
burning in its origins but a dark transparency,
and it arrives like another her, again and again.

I too am a window. In August, two people
among the dead look out of it. They do not know
the window is me. And I am what a window can wish.
To open endlessly because it is light,
and because it is a mirror, let the silver erase itself
and arrive and wait flawless on the glass,
and darken, and erase itself, like life, like death.

A Stranger

It rains here. Maybe you know that.
The first day of summer, it's raining –
pieces of water plummeting,
a set of pulleys lifting air. The trees
coming down the dark mountain
to carry clouds. I'm speaking to a stranger.
You're actually no longer alive.
Still, I can't speak to anyone else. What
would you have said? "You live in rain."
Yes, it's conditioned my sight. Before
whatever I say is sluiced away, I will say
I love what sluices it away. It was you
who said you were speaking to a stranger.
All your letters. The small, old-fashioned
envelopes, writing paper. You said,
because of this drug or that drug,
half the time you were unable to tell
whether you were awake or asleep.
I can't tell now whether certain words
are yours or mine. It keeps on raining.
The great piles of river boulders, the wild
driftwood that still rolls onto the shore,
even the cedar and fir trees, are shapes
the rain makes as it pours and is a place.
You are a stranger. And I remember detail
after detail of you. The faint shadows
under the archways of your eyes. Your
black jeans, your boots. I can't speak to you.
I address the rain. And all the time
a stranger finds and fills me. That stranger
is whose mouth is at your ear. I can now
say everything that anyone can say
to another. The rain will be a stranger
and will speak to itself through you and me.

The Smoke and the Fire

Smoke, a horse of ash turning in the air.
Late summer fire somewhere near. I find out
a woman I loved has been dead for years,
and the fire that is birds, animals, trees,
blazes up from end to end, then vanishes.
Returns instantaneously, the world
riding through the world. The slow fire of my flesh
pauses, watches, and I see the flame she was
leap, rise, soar toward death. See that the flame
holds her memory and what love she knew,
and is a chariot, a vehicle
of swerving golden light. The grey-black smoke
as soon hovers wildly there, a dark mare
among the chariots of the Pharaoh.
It rears, is gone, then the overturned world ·
comes back again, burning. The world is its own
oldest road. The wheels of its flames spin
spokes that take the wheels rotating back
to the first fire. The fire dies, is reborn,
as many times a day as there are days
to count since the first day. The chariots,
charioteers, stallions, come driving
out of the fire. And the living smoke that lies
within the light of the snapping out flames
displays itself and momentarily
moves shifting free of the royal mouthpiece,
the harness, yoke, sets of reins and blinders
before it leaves. No accusatory cry
among the elements earth, air, water, fire.
Is she the chariot or the dark mare
among the chariots? The chariot
of my flesh in which I must follow her,
or the floating smoke? The flame vanishes,
taking her with it on its way elsewhere,
then the smoke vanishes, taking with it
all the roads on its way to no haven,
only into the world, where all ash goes.

Cana

When the guests gather near, and the two of them share the wine,
the guests behold them, they behold many brides and bridegrooms,

they see all couples as a single couple.
When they see the glass being flung to the ground,

they watch it shatter into the bride and bridegroom they know,
and into the miracle of infinite repair –

and out of the guests' mouths come animal cries.
When evening arrives and the darkness expands,

in the guests' eyes the wedding light contracts –
and they witness the light's trial and acquittal.

And when the guests lack wine, and the servers
are instructed to fill with water the standing stone jars,

where they believe the water will lie deep and clear,
deep and clear as the eyes of the newly wedded ones,

they look and see the water changed into wine.
That is when wine begins to flow again as if for the first time,

and the celebration continues, the canopy fluttering like an eyelid.
In the deep mirror of the wine the wedding continues.

Absence

I am here. I feel as if I am waiting.
Whatever this place is, it is inhabited
by the wrong people. The face in the mirror –
not really one I know. Eyes closed, falling
asleep, I repeat prayers about kingdoms
coming and wills being done, a valley
of the shadow of death, cups running over.
I am here, and as long as I am alive
I can believe you are here. It is a theory.
I want to reconstruct certain times
from the details I find on a roadside
in the dark nowhere in my head. While
I am asleep I want the right details
to fit together in the right whole. I stay
alive because that way I can try to find you.

I find you. You are there in my dreaming,
dismantling yourself limb by limb until
you lie in front of me in pieces. If I die
I will not see this. You did not look back,
you defiantly told me once. Not ever.
When I was the one looking far ahead.
All the way to now. I knew that soon
enough I would not see your face again.
Now I say any prayer I have at hand.
In case it might work. I say the words.
I want to wake with you somewhere –
at a table across from me, a cup of coffee
in your hands, living mouth, living eyes.

Years ago now, you dismantled yourself.
If I stay alive and keep trying to put you
together again, I may make a dream stay
in my waking. I may see you when I look
straight into nothing but the hurrying light
of day, the arrested light of things, you
looking out through me into your absence.

A List

Once, I would make certain my name
did not appear in any directory. Now
I dream I am back in different times and places,
and the people I remember I loved
are not there, and the places not at all
as they were, and it is as if I have belonged
to some underground organization
set up to allow no member
to betray another – no member ever
knowing who his associates actually are.

Now I agree to be listed, I ask to be listed –
and hope that this will make it easy to find me.
And now I dream of a list. On it
everything I and those I have been with
have ever truly felt or done is recorded
in the clearest detail. In the same dream
is a man who walks alongside me and knows
nothing but the entire list by heart,
and will recite it to the moment I die,
and then he too will disappear.

Thirst

The card you gave me, your small handwriting
on the back – is gone. But the deep black ink
of the artist's drawing pen stayed with me,
and the ancient couplets became the dark
that holds the living organs, the same dark
through which the deer runs, giving off thin smoke
as it seeks the stream. I enter that dark
now in sleep, and I hear you: *What you bear,*
I will like my own body bear and tend.
I will be the breath in the animal
that pants and whose heart chants through it,
that burns like the one fire in a night camp,
and that departs from the night where it thirsts
to find the waters when the sun appears.

All this time you have been the one in me
who arrives and stands with me at the stream,
where I seem to sleep instantly, my breath
unseen rungs that lower me down. The wound
in the deer is memory of waters
and allows the deer to bow, drink. Ripples
in the quick flowing melt me. Whatever
my desire is, here it finds change. I wake
burning but becoming dark and more dark
and moving through the touch of water. Wake
within pure explanation: I am what
I come to, and always I come to you –
to know you is to want like fire, water,
to remember the first fire, first waters.

Double-Flute

Buried sounds of music and singing
flow from the hollow of the double-flute
and the throat and lips. The air, a radiant
grave, weeps. The invisible figure laughs.

Acknowledgements & Notes

With a Greek Pen
Several of the poems here first appeared in the following
literary magazines: *The Antigonish Review, Canadian Literature, The
Fiddlehead, Grain, The Malahat Review, Northern Poetry Review*, and
Poetry Canada Review. Some of the poems were included in the
anthologies *In Fine Form* (Polestar Press, 2005) and *White Ink*
(Demeter Press, 2007). Some of the poems were published in
Greek translation in the anthologies *Foreign Language Poems on
Thessaloniki* (Kedros Publishers, Athens, 1997), *Into a Foreign
Tongue Goes Our Grief: Poems On or After Cavafy* (Bilieto Publishers,
Peania, 2000), *Thessaloniki: A City in Literature* (Metaixmo
Publishers, Athens, 2001), and *On Travelling Through Greece with
Poets and Writers*: http://key-em.blogspot.ca/2007/10/67.html. A
number of the poems appeared in *The Fifth Window* (Thistledown
Press, 2000), *A Tunisian Notebook* (Seraphim Editions, 2002),
House Built of Rain (Harbour Publishing, 2003), *The Human Shore*
(Harbour Publishing, 2006), and *Birds, Metals, Stones & Rain*
(Harbour Publishing, 2013).

Lazarus' Songs to Mary Magdalene
These poems first appeared in *The Fifth Window* (Thistledown
Press, 2000).

Lazarus is meant here as a symbolic composite figure. Lazarus,
Jesus and Mary Magdalene are all associated psychic realities and
aspects of one and the same imaginary personality.

from Book of the Dark Dove
The quotations heading these pieces are from the following
sections of *The Song of Songs* (in order of appearance):
"My mother's sons were angry with me ..." – 1: 6
"Where do you pasture?" – 1:7
"You are beautiful, my love ..." – 1:15
"He brought me into the wine-house ..." – 2:4-5

"O my love, in the crannies of the cliff ..." – 2:4
"Catch us the little foxes ..." – 2:15
"Upon my couch I sought him whom I love ..." – 3:1
"When I found the one I love ..." – 3:4
"You have ravished my heart, my sister, my bride ..." – 4:9
"The watchmen who patrol the city found me ..." – 5:7
"My beloved has gone down to his garden ..." – 6:2
"Turn, turn, O Shulamite ..." – 6:13
"The locks of your head are like purple ..." – 7:5
"I would give you spiced wine to drink ..." – 8:2
"Let me be a seal upon your heart ..." – 8:6

The last few lines of "My brothers of the earth ..." (beginning
I am the first and the last ...) are a quotation from the Gnostic text
The Thunder: Perfect Mind.

Double-Flute

Some of these poems first appeared in the following
publications:
Branch Magazine – "Thirst"
Existere – "Candy"
The Maynard – "Pitcher"
The Companions Series (Broadsheet #7, High Ground Press, 2008)
– "A List"

My deep gratitude to Allan Briesmaster for his editing of this
book.

Other Quattro Poetry Books

Night Vision by Christopher Levenson
Pin Pricks by Phlip Arima
Under the Mulberry Tree edited by James Deahl
Come Cold River by Karen Connelly
Beyond Mudtown by Rob Rolfe
And the cat says... by Susan L. Helwig
Against the Flight of Spring by Allan Briesmaster
The Rules of the Game by Ludwig Zeller
Too Much Love by Gianna Patriarca
parterre by elías carlo
Night-Eater by Patricia Young
Fermata by Dennison Smith
Little Empires by Robert Colman
nunami by Barbara Landry
One False Move by Tim Conley
Where the Terror Lies by Chantel Lavoie
Something Small To Carry Home by Isa Milman
jumping in the asylum by Patrick Friesen
Without Blue by Chris D'Iorio
When the Earth by Lisa Young
And tell tulip the summer by Allan Graubard
Book of Disorders by Luciano Iacobelli
Saugeen by Rob Rolfe
Strong Bread by Giovanna Riccio
Rough Wilderness by Rosemary Aubert
hold the note by Domenico Capilongo
syrinx and systole by Matthew Remski
Sew Him Up by Beatriz Hausner
Psychic Geographies and Other Topics by Gregory Betts
The Sylvia Hotel Poems by George Fetherling
Ten Thousand Miles Between Us by Rocco de Giacomo
A River at Night by Paul Zemokhol
This Is How I Love You by Barbara Landry
Looking at Renaissance Paintings by Caroline Morgan Di Giovanni
The Hawk by Rob Rolfe
My Etruscan Face by Gianna Patriarca
Garden Variety edited by Lily Contento
MIC CHECK edited by David Silverberg
Evidence by Samuel Andreyev
Interstellar by Allan Briesmaster